The Power of Instagram Marketing

Marketing

How to Use the Platform to Grow Your
Business and Increase Sales

Henry John

DEDICATION

To my wife Marian, who has always been my rock and my biggest supporter. Your unwavering love and encouragement have given me the strength to pursue my dreams and share my knowledge with the world. This book would not have been possible without your constant support and belief in me. Thank you for being my partner in life and in business. I dedicate this book to you with all my heart.

CONTENTS

1 INTRODUCTION

Instagram is a social media platform that has exploded in popularity over the past few years, with over one billion active users worldwide. As a result, it has become a powerful tool for businesses looking to reach a wide audience and build their brand.

Instagram marketing involves using the platform to promote products, services, or content to a target audience. This can include posting photos and videos, using Instagram Stories and Reels, and collaborating with influencers to reach a wider audience. The ultimate goal of Instagram marketing is to increase brand awareness, generate leads, and drive sales.

One of the benefits of Instagram marketing is that it allows businesses to engage with their audience in a more visual and personal way. By using eye-catching photos and videos, businesses can capture the attention of potential customers and showcase their products or services creatively and engagingly.

However, to succeed in Instagram marketing, businesses need to have a clear strategy and understand the platform's algorithms and best practices. This includes identifying their target audience, creating high-quality content, using hashtags and geotags effectively, and analyzing their performance metrics to continually improve their approach.

If you want to get started, here are a few tips on how to get started

https://instagram.com/ojoekeyz?igshid=ZDdkNTZiNTM=

henrycash0713@gmail.com

2 CREATE AN INSTAGRAM BUSINESS ACCOUNT

Instagram has become one of the most popular social media platforms for businesses to reach and engage with their target audience. With over 1 billion active monthly users, Instagram provides businesses with a vast audience to showcase their products and services, build brand awareness, and connect with potential customers. However, to make the most of Instagram's marketing potential, businesses need to have a dedicated Instagram Business Account.

Creating an Instagram Business Account is a crucial first step in leveraging the power of this social media platform. It offers several features that are not available on personal accounts, including access to Instagram Insights, which provides valuable data about your audience. Instagram Insights allows you to track engagement metrics, follower demographics, post reach, and other key performance indicators, which can help you refine your content and improve your marketing strategy.

Another significant advantage of having an Instagram Business Account is the ability to run Instagram Ads. Instagram Ads are a powerful tool for businesses to reach a broader audience beyond their current followers. With Instagram Ads, you can target specific demographics, interests, behaviors, and more, making it easier to get your content in front of the right people. Instagram Ads can help drive traffic to your website, increase brand awareness, and generate leads and sales.

In addition to the practical benefits, having an Instagram Business Account can also have psychological benefits for your brand. By having a dedicated business account, you appear more professional and trustworthy to potential customers. People are more likely to engage with businesses with a polished and cohesive online presence, and an Instagram Business Account can help you achieve this.

To create an Instagram Business Account, you'll need to have a Facebook Page for your business. Once you've created a Facebook Page, you can easily connect it to your Instagram account and switch to a Business Account in the Instagram settings. From there, you can customize your profile, add your contact information, and start posting content that resonates with your target audience.

Overall, creating an Instagram Business Account is an essential first step to making money on the platform. With access to Instagram Insights and the ability to run ads, you can reach a larger audience, track your engagement, and drive more leads and sales. Moreover, having a business account makes your brand appear more professional and trustworthy to potential customers, which can help you build a stronger online presence and increase your chances of success on Instagram. So, if you're looking to make money on Instagram, start by creating a business account and developing a robust marketing strategy that resonates with your target audience.

3 BUILD AN ENGAGED AUDIENCE

Building an engaged audience on Instagram is an ongoing process that requires consistent effort and attention. Here are some additional strategies that can help you build and maintain an engaged audience on Instagram:

Be consistent with your posting schedule: Consistency is key to building an engaged audience on Instagram. Post consistently and at optimal times to reach your audience when they're most active on the platform. You can use Instagram Insights to determine the best times to post based on your audience's activity.

Use Instagram's features to your advantage: Instagram offers a range of features that can help you build engagement with your audience, including Instagram Stories, Reels, and IGTV. Use these features to showcase your brand's personality and values, share behind-the-scenes content, and provide value to your followers.

Use user-generated content (UGC): User-generated content is a powerful way to build engagement with your audience and showcase your brand's social proof. Encourage your followers to share their own content using your branded hashtags, and feature UGC on your Instagram feed and Stories.

Host Instagram Live sessions: Instagram Live sessions are a great way to engage with your audience in real time and provide value to your followers. Use Instagram Live to host Q&A sessions, share industry insights, and provide behind-the-scenes content.

Run Instagram Ads: Instagram Ads can help you reach a larger audience and drive more leads and sales. Use Instagram Ads to promote your content, products, or services, and target your ads based on demographics, interests, and behaviors.

Analyze your performance: Regularly analyzing your Instagram performance is essential to understanding what content resonates with your audience and how you can improve your engagement. Use Instagram Insights to track your metrics, such as engagement rates, follower growth, and reach, and adjust your strategy accordingly.

In conclusion, building an engaged audience on Instagram is a critical component of a successful marketing strategy. By understanding your audience, creating high-quality content, engaging with your followers, collaborating with other brands and influencers, and utilizing Instagram's features, you can build a strong and engaged audience that supports your brand's growth and success. Remember that building an audience takes time and effort, but with persistence and dedication, you can achieve your goals on Instagram.

4 SELL PRODUCTS ON INSTAGRAM

Selling products on Instagram is an effective way to reach a large audience and increase sales for your business. To be successful in selling on Instagram, you need to have a clear strategy and use the right tools and techniques to promote your products.

One of the first steps to selling on Instagram is to have a business account. This type of account provides you with access to various features that can help you promote your products, including Instagram Insights, which provides you with valuable data about your audience and their engagement with your content. Additionally, you can use Instagram Ads to reach a larger audience and target your ads based on demographics, interests, behaviors, and more.

To set up an Instagram shop, you need to meet certain requirements, such as having a physical product to sell, complying with Instagram's merchant policies, and linking your account to a Facebook page. Once you meet these requirements, you can create a product catalog and add your products to the shop. You can also use Instagram's product tags to tag your products in your posts and stories, making it easier for your audience to discover and purchase your products.

In addition to the Instagram Shop, you can use Instagram Stories to promote your products. Stories are a great way to showcase your products and engage with your audience. You can use features like polls, quizzes, and stickers to create interactive stories that drive engagement and sales. You can also use Instagram's Swipe Up feature to add links to your stories, directing your audience to your website or the product page.

When creating content to promote your products, it is important to focus on quality and relevance. Use high-quality images and videos that showcase your products in the best light, and write engaging captions that provide information about your products and encourage your audience to take action. You can also use user-generated content to showcase your products in real-life situations, which can help build trust and credibility with your audience.

Another effective way to promote your products on Instagram is to collaborate with influencers and other businesses in your niche. This can help you reach a larger audience and build credibility with your target market. Look for influencers and businesses that share your values and target audience, and create content or promotions that align with your brand and product offering.

There are numerous lucrative products that you can sell on Instagram. However, the choice of what to sell depends on your target audience and your niche. Here are some ideas for products that you can sell on Instagram:

Fashion items: Fashion is a popular niche on Instagram, and you can sell clothing, accessories, and jewelry. You can also target specific niches within fashion, such as eco-friendly or sustainable fashion.

Beauty products: The beauty industry is thriving on Instagram, and you can sell makeup, skincare products, and hair care products. You can also target specific niches, such as natural or organic beauty products.

Home decor: Home decor is a popular niche on Instagram, and you can sell items such as wall art, furniture, and home accessories. You can also target specific niches within home decor, such as bohemian or minimalistic styles.

Fitness products: Fitness is a growing niche on Instagram, and you can sell fitness equipment, supplements, and apparel. You can also target specific niches within fitness, such as yoga or CrossFit.

Tech gadgets: Tech gadgets are always popular, and you can sell items such as headphones, phone cases, and smartwatches. You can also target specific niches within tech, such as gaming or photography.

Pet products: Pet owners are a passionate audience on Instagram, and you can sell pet food, toys, and accessories. You can also target specific niches within the pet industry, such as eco-friendly or organic pet products.

Personalized items: Personalized items, such as customized phone cases, jewelry, and clothing, are always in demand on Instagram. You can offer personalized items that cater to different niches and interests.

When choosing what to sell on Instagram, it's important to consider your target audience, your niche, and your passion for the product. By choosing a product that you are passionate about and that resonates with your target audience, you can create a successful Instagram business.

In conclusion, selling products on Instagram can be a powerful tool for increasing sales and growing your business. By setting up an Instagram shop, using Instagram Stories, creating high-quality content, and collaborating with influencers and other businesses, you can reach a larger audience and build a successful e-commerce business on the platform. Remember to stay consistent with your posting schedule and engage with your audience regularly to build trust and foster a strong community around your brand.

5 PROMOTE AFFILIATE PRODUCTS

Affiliate marketing on Instagram is a great way to monetize your content and earn passive income. It's a win-win situation for both the affiliate marketer and the company selling the product. For the company, it's an opportunity to increase its sales and reach a wider audience through the affiliate marketer's social media following. For the affiliate marketer, it's an opportunity to earn a commission for promoting products they believe in and that their audience would benefit from.

One of the advantages of affiliate marketing on Instagram is that it's relatively easy to get started. You don't need to have your own products, inventory, or even a website. All you need is a strong social media presence and the ability to create high-quality content that resonates with your audience.

To succeed with affiliate marketing on Instagram, it's important to find affiliate programs that align with your niche and audience. This means looking for products that are relevant to your followers and that you believe in. For example, if you have a fitness-focused Instagram account, you might look for affiliate programs that sell workout gear, supplements, or healthy snacks.

Once you've found an affiliate program that you want to promote, you'll need to sign up and get your unique affiliate link. This link is what you'll use to promote the product on Instagram, and it allows the company to track sales generated through your link so they can pay you a commission.

When promoting affiliate products on Instagram, it's important to be transparent about the fact that you're using affiliate links. This is required by law in many countries, including the United States. You can do this by including a disclosure statement in your post or by using Instagram's built-in "paid partnership" feature.

To maximize your success with affiliate marketing on Instagram, it's important to create high-quality content that engages your audience and showcases the product you're promoting in a positive light. This could include creating posts, stories, or even videos that highlight the features and benefits of the product.

Another important factor in affiliate marketing success is building trust with your audience. This means only promoting products that you truly believe in and that you think will benefit your followers. It also means being honest and transparent about your experiences with the product, both positive and negative.

In conclusion, affiliate marketing can be a lucrative way to make money on Instagram, but it requires effort and dedication to be successful. By finding affiliate programs that align with your niche, being transparent about your use of affiliate links, creating high-quality content, and building trust with your audience, you can build a successful affiliate marketing strategy on Instagram.

6 OFFER SPONSORED POSTS

Sponsored posts have become a popular way for influencers to monetize their content and collaborate with brands. As the popularity of Instagram continues to grow, more and more brands are looking to work with influencers to reach new audiences and promote their products or services.

To offer sponsored posts on Instagram, the first step is to build a significant following in your niche. This means creating high-quality content that resonates with your audience and using strategies like hashtags and engaging with your followers to reach new people. Building a loyal following takes time and effort, but it's essential for attracting brands and earning their trust.

Once you have a significant following, you can start reaching out to brands in your niche to offer sponsored posts. This can be done by sending them a message or email explaining your services and what you can offer in terms of promoting their products or services. It's important to be clear about your reach and engagement rates so that brands can see the value in working with you.

When creating sponsored posts, it's important to disclose that you're being paid for the post. This is required by law in many countries, including the United States, and failure to disclose sponsored content can result in penalties or fines. You can disclose that a post is sponsored by including a sponsored tag or hashtag in your post, or by using Instagram's built-in "paid partnership" feature.

The fee for each sponsored post or campaign will depend on a number of factors, including your reach and engagement rates, the brand's budget, and the type of content you're creating. You can negotiate the fee with the brand based on these factors to ensure that you're being fairly compensated for your work.

To maximize the success of your sponsored posts, it's important to create high-quality content that engages your audience and showcases the brand's products or services in a positive light. This could include creating posts, stories, or even videos that highlight the features and benefits of the product. The content should be authentic and reflect your personal brand, while also meeting the expectations of the brand you're collaborating with.

Overall, offering sponsored posts on Instagram can be a lucrative way to monetize your content and collaborate with brands in your niche. By building a significant following, reaching out to brands, and creating high-quality sponsored content that engages your audience, you can build a successful business as an influencer on Instagram. However, it's important to be transparent about your sponsored posts and to ensure that your content is authentic and aligns with your personal brand.

7 CREATE AND SELL ONLINE COURSES

Online learning has become increasingly popular in recent years, especially with the COVID-19 pandemic accelerating the shift toward remote work and online education. Instagram, as one of the largest social media platforms, provides a unique opportunity for educators and experts to promote their courses and engage with their audience.

If you have a particular skill or expertise that you think would be valuable to others, creating and selling online courses can be a great way to monetize your knowledge. Whether you're an expert in cooking, photography, marketing, entrepreneurship, or any other niche, there's likely a demand for your expertise from people who are looking to learn and improve their skills.

To create an online course, you'll need to start by planning out your content and structuring it into a series of lessons or modules. You can use a variety of tools to create your course, including video tutorials, text-based lessons, and interactive quizzes and assignments. It's important to make sure that your course is engaging, informative, and easy to follow so that your students get the most out of their learning experience.

Once you've created your course, you can sell it through your own website or a third-party platform like Udemy or Skillshare. These platforms provide a convenient way to sell and distribute your course to a large audience, but they may also take a percentage of your earnings in exchange for their services.

To promote your course on Instagram, you can use a variety of strategies to engage with your audience and build excitement around your content. One effective approach is to use Instagram Live to provide a sneak peek of your course content and interact with your followers in real time. You can also use Instagram Stories to share behind-the-scenes glimpses of your course creation process and build anticipation among your audience.

When pricing your course, it's important to strike a balance between offering value to your audience and ensuring that you're fairly compensated for your time and effort. You can set a price based on the amount of content and the level of expertise you're providing, but it's important to be mindful of the market and to research similar courses in your niche to ensure that your pricing is competitive.

Overall, online courses can be a lucrative way to monetize your knowledge and expertise, especially if you have a loyal following that values your content. By creating high-quality content, promoting your course on Instagram, and engaging with your audience, you can build a successful business as an online course creator.

8 OFFER FREELANCE SERVICES

Freelancing has become increasingly popular in recent years, and with the rise of social media, it's easier than ever to promote and offer your services to potential clients. Instagram, in particular, is a powerful platform to showcase your skills and connect with people who are looking for your expertise.

To start offering your freelance services on Instagram, you'll need to first identify your niche and the services that you want to offer. This could be anything from copywriting and graphic design to web development and social media management. The key is to choose a niche that you're passionate about and that aligns with your skills and experience.

Once you've identified your niche, you can create a post showcasing your portfolio and promoting your services. Your post should include examples of your work, testimonials from satisfied clients, and information about your pricing and availability. It's also important to include relevant hashtags to help potential clients find your post.

To reach a wider audience, you can use Instagram's features to engage with your audience and provide more details about your services. For example, you can use Instagram Stories to share behind-the-scenes glimpses of your work and provide tips and insights for your followers. You can also use Instagram Live to answer questions and provide real-time feedback to your audience.

Networking is also a crucial component of building a successful freelance business on Instagram. You can join relevant Facebook groups or LinkedIn groups, attend industry events and conferences, and reach out to other professionals in your niche to build relationships and find new clients.

When offering freelance services on Instagram, it's important to showcase your expertise and provide value to your clients. This could include offering a free consultation, providing high-quality work that exceeds your client's expectations, and maintaining open communication throughout the project. By building trust and delivering results, you can build a loyal client base and attract new business through word-of-mouth referrals.

Ultimately, offering freelance services on Instagram can be a lucrative way to build your business and grow your client base. By creating high-quality content, promoting your services on Instagram, and building relationships with potential clients, you can build a successful career as a freelancer in your niche.

9 MONETIZE YOUR INSTAGRAM ACCOUNT

Since Instagram has become one of the most popular social media platforms in the world, with over 1 billion active users mentioned earlier. It's not surprising that many people have taken advantage of this platform to make money. If you have a popular Instagram account with a large following, you can monetize it in various ways.

One of the most common ways to monetize your Instagram account is by charging for membership or offering exclusive content. For example, you can create a paid subscription service that provides exclusive access to your content, such as behind-the-scenes footage, tutorials, or early access to new products or services. You can also charge for access to a private group or community on Instagram, where members can connect and interact with each other.

Another way to monetize your Instagram account is by using it to promote your products or services. You can use Instagram to showcase your products, highlight their features, and provide information about their benefits. You can also create sponsored posts for other brands or businesses that align with your values and appeal to your audience. These sponsored posts can generate income through affiliate marketing, where you earn a commission for each sale that is made through your referral link.

To make the most of your Instagram account and attract a larger audience, focus on creating high-quality content that resonates with your audience and provides value. This includes using high-quality images and videos, writing compelling captions, and engaging with your followers through comments and direct messages. You can also use hashtags and tagging to increase your reach and visibility on Instagram.

In addition to creating high-quality content, it's important to build relationships with your followers and engage with them regularly. This includes responding to comments, liking and commenting on their posts, and hosting live events or Q&A sessions to interact with your audience directly. By building a strong relationship with your followers, you can increase their loyalty and trust, which can lead to higher engagement and conversions.

Another way to monetize your Instagram account is by partnering with other influencers or brands. You can collaborate with other influencers to create joint content or work with brands to promote their products. These partnerships can generate income through sponsored posts, affiliate marketing, or other arrangements.

You can also monetize your Instagram account by selling your own products or services. For example, if you have a strong personal brand, you can create and sell merchandise or digital products, such as ebooks or online courses. You can also offer coaching or consulting services to your followers.

Finally, it's important to stay up-to-date with the latest trends and changes on Instagram. The platform is constantly evolving, and new features and opportunities for monetization are emerging all the time. By staying informed and adaptable, you can stay ahead of the curve and continue to grow and monetize your Instagram account.

In conclusion, monetizing your Instagram account requires a strategic approach and consistent effort. By creating high-quality content, building relationships with your audience, and using the platform to promote your products or services, you can turn your Instagram account into a profitable business venture. Whether you're charging for membership, partnering with brands, or selling your own products, there are many ways to monetize your Instagram account and turn your passion into profit.

10 RUN INSTAGRAM ADS

Social media has become a crucial marketing tool for businesses to connect with their target audience and promote their products or services in recent times. With over 1 billion active users, There is no wonder why Instagram is one of the most popular social media platforms, making it an excellent platform for businesses to reach a wider audience. Running Instagram ads is a cost-effective way to boost your brand's visibility and drive conversions on the platform.

Instagram ads come in a variety of formats, including photo, video, carousel, and story ads. You can use these formats to showcase your products, highlight their features, and provide information about their benefits. With Instagram's ad targeting capabilities, you can create targeted ads that reach a specific demographic and location, making it easier to connect with potential customers who are more likely to be interested in your brand.

To get started with Instagram ads, you'll need to set up an advertising account on Facebook Ads Manager. This will allow you to create and manage your ads, set your budget, and track your performance. When creating your Instagram ad, you'll need to define your target audience, choose your ad format, and set your budget and bidding strategy.

One of the most crucial aspects of running Instagram ads is tracking your ad performance and adjusting your strategy accordingly. Instagram's ad manager provides detailed metrics, such as reach, impressions, clicks, and conversions, that you can use to measure the effectiveness of your ads. Based on these metrics, you can refine your targeting, adjust your ad format, and optimize your budget to get the best results.

However, it's important to note that creating successful Instagram ads requires more than just targeting and budgeting. Your ads should align with your brand's visual identity and tone of voice to create a cohesive and engaging experience for your audience. It's crucial to ensure that your ads are visually appealing, relevant, and provide value to your target audience.

To make the most of your Instagram ad strategy, it's essential to also consider the overall aesthetics and messaging of your Instagram account. Your ads should complement your organic content and align with your brand's identity to create a consistent and recognizable experience for your audience.

In conclusion, Instagram ads are a powerful marketing tool that can help businesses reach a wider audience and promote their products or services. By creating targeted ads, tracking your performance, and refining your strategy, you can optimize your ad spending and drive conversions on the platform. However, it's important to remember that successful Instagram ads require more than just targeting and budgeting. By creating cohesive and engaging content, you can build a strong brand presence on the platform and connect with your audience in a meaningful way.

11 CREATE SPONSORED CONTENT

Sponsored content has become an increasingly popular marketing strategy for brands to reach new audiences and promote their products or services. If you have a blog or website, you can leverage your online presence and create sponsored content for brands, sharing it on Instagram to reach a wider audience.

Sponsored content is a form of advertising where a brand pays you to create content that promotes its products or services. This can take many forms, such as blog posts, social media posts, videos, or podcasts. Instagram is a particularly popular platform for sponsored content, as it has a large and engaged user base.

To create sponsored content, you'll need to find brands that align with your values and interests and are willing to pay for sponsored posts. You can reach out to brands directly or sign up for influencer marketing platforms that connect you with brands looking for sponsored content creators.

Once you've found a brand that you want to work with, you'll need to create content that promotes their products or services in a way that's authentic and engaging. This can be a creative challenge, as you'll need to balance the brand's messaging with your own personal brand and style. It's important to ensure that your sponsored content aligns with your values and interests and that it provides value to your audience.

When creating sponsored content for Instagram, you'll need to include a sponsored tag to disclose that you're being paid for the post. This is a requirement set by the Federal Trade Commission (FTC) to ensure transparency and disclosure in sponsored content. You can use hashtags like #sponsored, #ad, or #paid to indicate that a post is sponsored.

When it comes to pricing sponsored content, you can charge a fee for each sponsored post, depending on your reach and engagement metrics. You can negotiate with brands to determine the fee that works for both parties. It's important to have clear communication with brands regarding your rates, expectations, and deliverables.

In conclusion, sponsored content on Instagram is a great way for bloggers and website owners to monetize their online presence and reach a wider audience. By creating authentic and engaging content that promotes brands' products or services, you can build relationships with brands, grow your following, and generate income. It's important to ensure that your sponsored content aligns with your values and principles.

12 OFFER COACHING OR CONSULTING SERVICES

Offering coaching or consulting services on Instagram can be an excellent way to monetize your expertise and knowledge. Instagram, with its large user base, presents a unique opportunity for businesses and individuals to reach a wider audience and connect with potential clients. Whether you have years of experience in business, marketing, social media, or any other niche, there are likely people who could benefit from your guidance and advice.

To start offering coaching or consulting services on Instagram, you first need to establish your brand and create a strong online presence. You can achieve this by creating a compelling Instagram profile that showcases your expertise, experience, and what sets you apart from other coaches or consultants. Your profile should have a clear bio that describes your services, your niche, and how you can help your clients. It's also essential to have a professional headshot as your profile picture and a visually appealing feed that aligns with your brand.

Once you have a strong online presence, you can start promoting your coaching or consulting services. Creating a post that clearly explains what you offer and how you can help your clients achieve their goals is an excellent place to start. This post should be visually appealing and have a strong call-to-action (CTA) that encourages potential clients to reach out to you. You can also include testimonials from past clients to give potential clients an idea of what they can expect when working with you.

To reach potential clients, you can use relevant hashtags to increase the visibility of your posts. You can also directly message people who you think could benefit from your services. Another strategy is to run paid ads on Instagram to reach a broader audience.

When working with clients, it's crucial to be clear about what they can expect from your coaching or consulting services. This may include regular check-ins, personalized advice and guidance, and access to your network of contacts and resources. You should also be upfront about your rates and any other fees or expenses associated with your services. Being transparent about your pricing will help you avoid misunderstandings with clients and ensure that you get paid fairly for your services.

It's also important to prioritize building relationships with your clients. You should strive to create a safe and supportive environment where clients feel comfortable sharing their goals and challenges with you. Regular communication and feedback are also essential to ensure that you're meeting your client's needs and expectations.

Overall, offering coaching or consulting services on Instagram can be an excellent way to share your knowledge and expertise with others while earning money. With the right approach and a commitment to providing value to your clients, you can build a successful coaching or consulting business on Instagram.

13 SELL DIGITAL PRODUCTS

In today's digital age, selling digital products has become a popular and profitable way for individuals to monetize their online presence. If you have a blog or website, you can create digital products such as ebooks, templates, or printables and sell them on platforms like Instagram. Instagram is an ideal platform for selling digital products because it has a large user base and allows for easy promotion and sharing of products through posts, stories, and highlights.

One of the most significant advantages of selling digital products is that they are low-cost to create and have high-profit margins. Unlike physical products, there are no production or shipping costs associated with creating and selling digital products. Once you have created your digital product, it can be sold an unlimited number of times, which means you can earn passive income without having to continually create new products. Additionally, digital products can be easily updated and improved based on customer feedback, ensuring that your products remain relevant and valuable to your audience.

Creating digital products can also provide added value to your followers and customers. If you have a blog or website, you likely have a niche audience that is interested in your expertise and insights. By creating digital products that cater to their specific needs, you can provide them with additional value and establish yourself as an authority in your niche. This, in turn, can lead to increased trust and loyalty from your audience, which can translate into more sales and revenue.

To successfully sell digital products on Instagram, it's important to create a cohesive and visually appealing feed that showcases your products and establishes your brand identity. You can use Instagram's features such as hashtags, stories, and highlights to promote your products and engage with your followers. It's also essential to understand your audience and what they are looking for in a digital product. This will help you create products that are tailored to their needs and interests, increasing the likelihood of making a sale.

Another important aspect of selling digital products on Instagram is pricing. You want to ensure that your pricing is competitive and reflects the value of your products. You may want to consider offering discounts or promotions to incentivize purchases, especially for new product launches or during holidays or special events.

Finally, it's important to have a customer-centric approach when selling digital products on Instagram. This means providing excellent customer service, responding to customer inquiries in a timely manner, and offering refunds or exchanges if necessary. By prioritizing the needs and satisfaction of your customers, you can build a loyal customer base and increase the likelihood of repeat purchases.

In conclusion, selling digital products on Instagram can be a lucrative way to monetize your online content and provide value to your followers. With the right approach, you can create high-quality digital products that resonate with your audience and establish yourself as a leader in your niche. By understanding your audience, creating visually appealing content, and prioritizing customer satisfaction, you can build a successful and profitable digital product business on Instagram.

14 PARTICIPATE IN PAID SURVEYS

Participating in paid surveys is an excellent way to earn some extra cash without having to leave the comfort of your home. With the increasing popularity of social media platforms like Instagram, more and more companies are turning to these platforms to advertise their survey opportunities and reach a broader audience. Instagram has become an excellent resource for finding survey companies that offer paid survey opportunities.

Paid surveys are a valuable tool for companies looking to gather information about their target audience and make informed decisions about their products and services. As a participant in paid surveys, you'll be asked to provide your opinions on a range of topics, such as product preferences, shopping habits, and advertising effectiveness. By sharing your insights, you'll help companies improve their offerings, and in return, you'll receive payment, which can be in the form of cash, gift cards, or other rewards.

Instagram is a popular platform for finding paid survey opportunities because it has a massive user base that includes a broad range of individuals from all walks of life. You can find survey companies that advertise their services on the platform by searching relevant hashtags or following accounts that specialize in sharing information about paid survey opportunities. Some survey companies also have their own Instagram pages where they post updates about new survey opportunities and payment options.

When searching for paid survey opportunities on Instagram, it's essential to do your research and make sure that you're signing up with a reputable company. Look for reviews and feedback from other participants to gauge the legitimacy and reliability of the company. You should also be aware of any potential risks or scams associated with paid surveys and take appropriate precautions to protect your personal information and earnings.

Participating in paid surveys on Instagram can be a simple and convenient way to earn some extra cash in your spare time. While it may not provide a full-time income, it can provide a steady stream of income that can help supplement your regular earnings. By finding reputable survey companies and being consistent with your participation, you can maximize your earnings and enjoy the benefits of being a paid survey participant.

In conclusion, participating in paid surveys on Instagram is an easy and accessible way to earn some extra money. By following the right accounts and doing your research, you can find reputable survey companies and earn money by sharing your opinions and insights. It's a great way to make use of your free time and earn some extra cash on the side.

15 OFFER INFLUENCER SERVICES

Influencer marketing has become one of the most popular ways for brands to promote their products and services. With the rise of social media, influencers have become a key players in this space, as they have the ability to reach a large and engaged audience. Instagram is one of the most popular platforms for influencer marketing, with over one billion active users, making it a powerful tool for brands to connect with potential customers.

If you have a popular Instagram account with a significant following, you can offer influencer services to brands looking to reach a wider audience. As an influencer, you have the ability to create sponsored content, promote products, or offer endorsements to your followers, providing brands with a unique opportunity to reach their target demographic in an authentic and engaging way.

When offering influencer services, it's important to establish your niche and ensure that your content aligns with the interests and values of your followers. This will help you attract brands that are a good fit for your audience and maintain a strong relationship with your followers. For example, if your Instagram account is focused on fitness, it's important to work with brands that promote healthy living and fitness-related products.

You should also be transparent about any sponsored content or endorsements, ensuring that your audience understands the nature of the partnership. This is not only important for legal reasons but also to maintain the trust and credibility you have built with your followers. Be honest about your opinions and experiences with the product or service you are promoting, as this will help build trust with your audience and increase the chances of them purchasing the product.

To find brands that are interested in working with influencers, you can reach out to companies directly or join influencer marketing networks. These networks connect influencers with brands looking for promotion, making it easier to find relevant opportunities and negotiate fair compensation. Some influencer marketing networks even offer tools and resources to help influencers create high-quality content and track their engagement and earnings.

Building relationships with brands is also important as it can lead to long-term partnerships and a sustainable income stream. It's important to work with brands that you believe in and genuinely enjoy using their products or services. This will help you create authentic and engaging content that resonates with your audience and builds trust with your followers.

In conclusion, offering influencer services on Instagram can be a lucrative way to monetize your social media presence and provide value to brands looking to reach a wider audience. By establishing your niche, creating high-quality content, and building strong relationships with your followers and brand partners, you can establish yourself as a successful influencer and enjoy the benefits of a sustainable income stream. However, it's important to remember that building an engaged audience and establishing yourself as a successful influencer takes time and effort.

16 SELL PHYSICAL PRODUCTS

Since Instagram has become an essential platform for businesses to promote their products and services. Based on the fact that the social media platform has over one billion monthly active users, making it an ideal place to showcase and sell physical products. Instagram is a visual platform, making it easier to showcase your products and attract potential customers.

If you have a physical product to sell, Instagram can be an effective tool to help you increase your reach and ultimately grow your business. However, to successfully sell physical products on Instagram, you need to establish a strong brand identity and create high-quality content that accurately represents your brand and products.

Creating high-quality content is essential in attracting potential customers and keeping your existing ones engaged. It's important to focus on taking attractive and well-lit photos of your products, writing accurate and engaging product descriptions, and using relevant hashtags to increase your visibility on the platform. By investing time and effort into creating high-quality content, you can attract potential buyers and establish a strong presence on Instagram.

Engaging with your followers and building relationships with your customers is also crucial to the success of your Instagram business. Responding to comments and direct messages, offering promotions and discounts, and sharing user-generated content are all effective ways to build a loyal customer base and increase sales over time.

Selling physical products on Instagram has several benefits for your business. It allows you to reach a wider audience without the overhead costs associated with traditional marketing and advertising. By leveraging Instagram's built-in audience and targeting capabilities, you can promote your products to a highly targeted group of potential customers, increasing the likelihood of making sales and generating revenue.

To maximize your success on Instagram, it's important to stay up-to-date with the latest trends and best practices in social media marketing. This may involve experimenting with different content formats, using data analytics to track your engagement and conversions, and collaborating with other brands and influencers to expand your reach and build your brand.

In addition, Instagram is constantly evolving, and it's important to stay up-to-date with the platform's latest features and updates. For instance, Instagram now has a shopping feature that allows businesses to tag products in their posts, making it easier for customers to make purchases without leaving the app.

Overall, selling physical products on Instagram can be a great way to reach a wider audience and increase your sales. By focusing on creating high-quality content, engaging with your followers, and staying up-to-date with the latest trends and best practices in social media marketing, you can establish a successful and sustainable business on Instagram.

IN CONCLUSION

In recent years, Instagram has emerged as a highly lucrative platform for individuals and businesses to monetize their presence and generate income. With its massive user base and powerful marketing tools, Instagram provides countless opportunities for making money in various ways, ranging from selling products and services to participating in paid opportunities.

To effectively monetize your presence on Instagram, it's important to first establish a strong foundation by creating an Instagram Business Account and building an engaged audience. This involves developing a clear brand identity, creating high-quality content, and using various tactics such as hashtags, influencer marketing, and collaborations to attract and retain followers.

Once you have established a strong presence on Instagram, you can begin exploring various monetization options, such as selling digital or physical products, offering services, or participating in paid opportunities such as sponsored content or paid surveys. Each of these options requires a unique approach, with its own set of best practices and strategies for success.

For example, selling digital products such as ebooks, templates, or printables requires a strong focus on creating high-quality content that is valuable and relevant to your audience. Offering influencer services, on the other hand, involves building strong relationships with brands and creating sponsored content that aligns with your niche and audience interests.

Regardless of the specific monetization strategy you choose, it's important to remain dedicated, consistent, and creative in your approach. This may involve staying up-to-date with the latest trends and best practices in social media marketing, experimenting with different content formats and strategies, and constantly engaging with your followers to build a loyal customer base.

In conclusion, Instagram has emerged as a powerful platform for making money in various ways. Whether you are an influencer, entrepreneur, or individual with a particular skill or expertise, there are countless opportunities available to monetize your presence on the platform. By staying focused, creative, and strategic in your approach, you can successfully turn your Instagram account into a source of income and achieve your financial goals.

ABOUT THE AUTHOR

The Power of Instagram Marketing is a comprehensive guide that will help you harness the power of Instagram to grow your business and increase sales. With over 1 billion active users, Instagram has become one of the most popular social media platforms for businesses to reach and engage with their target audience. In this book, you'll learn how to create a winning Instagram strategy, optimize your profile and content, use hashtags effectively, engage with your audience, and measure your success. With practical tips, real-world examples, and case studies, this book is a must-read for any business owner or marketer looking to leverage Instagram for business success. Whether you're a beginner or an experienced Instagram user, The Power of Instagram Marketing will help you take your Instagram game to the next level.

About the Author

Henry John is a new author who has written a groundbreaking book on the power of Instagram marketing. With a passion for helping businesses grow and increase sales, Henry has dedicated himself to mastering the art of social media promotion. And now, he's sharing his hard-earned insights with readers in his debut book, "The Power of Instagram Marketing: How to Use the Platform to Grow Your Business and Increase Sales".

With a friendly and accessible writing style, Henry breaks down the complexities of Instagram marketing into simple, actionable steps. Drawing on his years of experience in digital marketing and e-commerce, he offers practical tips and strategies for businesses of all sizes. From crafting the perfect Instagram bio to optimizing your hashtags and engaging with your followers, "The Power of Instagram Marketing" is the ultimate guide to taking your business to the next level.

As a beginner in the world of book writing, Henry poured his heart and soul into this project. And the result is a book that's informative, and insightful but also engaging, and enjoyable to read. So whether you're a seasoned marketer or just starting out, "The Power of Instagram Marketing" is a must-read for anyone looking to harness the power of social media to grow their business.

www.ingramcontent.com/pod-product-compliance
Lightning Source LLC
Chambersburg PA
CBHW070905220526
45466CB00005B/2135